I0155316

Not Me

poems about other women

by

Linda Ferguson

Finishing Line Press
Georgetown, Kentucky

Not Me

poems about other women

ACKNOWLEDGMENTS

Grateful acknowledgement is made to the editors of the following
publications in which these poems first appeared, sometimes in a different
form:

Human/Kind Journal: "Sally as a Drake"
Oregon Poetry Association's Anthology of Pandemic Poems: "Pandemic Mary"
OyeDrum: "Pilgrim's Progress"
Ponder Away Online Open-Mic: "Soolie and the Art of Being"
Sonic Boom Journal: "Hunter's Moon" and "Sally in a Tangerine"
VoiceCatcher Journal: "Nancy Drew's Fancy," "The Ride," "Sighs of the
Mermaid"
The Wild Word: "Venetia's Dream"

Also thank you to all the strong women in my life, from my grandmothers
and mother to my daughter and all the women I've met through my classes
and in Carole Murphy's writing group.

Publisher: Leah Huete de Maines
Editor: Christen Kincaid
Cover Art: Linda Ferguson
Author Photo: Fiona Ferguson
Cover Design: Elizabeth Maines McCleavy

Order online: www.finishinglinepress.com
also available on amazon.com

Author inquiries and mail orders:
Finishing Line Press
PO Box 1626
Georgetown, Kentucky 40324
USA

Table of Contents

I.

Emily Dickinson Was More than a White Dress

Let them glimpse
a wisp
of angel's breath
and a dove's furtive,
shadowed flap—

Barefoot,
my vowels beat
a labyrinth
(a dance!)
between hemlock
maple, birch and beech—

It's not the house
I won't leave.
It's the forest
of my imagining—

Nancy Drew's Fancy

It's not Ned I want,
obviously.

Bess
Bess
Bess—
always.

Skin of silk
and cream,
a girl who eats—
oh jeez,
touch me.

Chums
riding in the blue
convertible,
the breeze
tangling my titian hair,
our pinkies
nearly linked
on the leather seat.

Plump anticipation
of a moonlit search—
up the steep staircase,
down the dark hallway,
a glimpse of freckles
sprinkled like clues,
a shiver
and some giggling.

Already more
than amateurs—
Bess and me
sleuthing,
sinking our teeth
into this new
mystery.

Venetia's Dream

for Venetia Burney, the math-loving English girl who named Pluto

In class, I fly on the backs of winged numbers—
with computations, I can have my plum cake
and eat it too, both the thrill and the comfort
of equality—12 - 3, 8 + 1, 45 ÷ by 5—
so many ways to get to nine,
or any number that I like.

But even from my silver hill of symbols and signs,
I sense the warped orbit of fear and scratching here.
Running my finger over the raw letters carved
into my wooden desk, I trace the initials of a girl
I once saw trip a fellow student then
apologize with her lips shaped
in a honeysuckle smile.

Today our teacher drones about Plato's ethics while I braid
strands of my hair with the hair of the other girls—
bully, witness, victim—a woven rope to read
like braille and bruises when I can't sleep.

I hear a new planet has been found. Would life be better,
more fair, on the edge of the galaxy?

Maybe in places where only dim starlight shines,
appreciation for each pale ray is multiplied.

Pandemic Mary

The god that Mary says she doesn't believe in sends her a dream:
The doors of an empty commuter train are sliding open. On the platform,
people wear rubber masks: pig, zebra, elephant. No one steps onto the train.
The train leaves. Pig, zebra and elephant remain standing. As if waiting for a
bell to ring before they can be released.

Mary is on a sixth-story balcony. Instead of a railing, there's a row of sheep,
shifting on their hooves—back and forth, back and forth, like the sea. Mary
feels dizzy, her brain a puff of cloud in the breeze.

Mary wakes up with an odd heartbeat. Like a skimming, skipping stone
before it sinks.

It's Easter Sunday. Not her thing. (Scourge of thorns and the monotony of
jelly beans stuck between her teeth.)

Mary's mother loves Easter: chicks and bunnies, pastel prayers and the
slender throats of lilies.

Mary's mother lives alone.

Mary's mother has lived through the Depression, a World War, and her
brother quarantined, his adolescent limbs wrapped in strips of warm wet
wool to stave off paralysis from polio.

'That was nothing,' Mary's mother says on the phone, 'compared to this.'
Meaning today. Suffocation and empty streets.

That evening Mary kneels on the floor with scissors and scraps of blue paper.
She cuts the paper into strips then weaves them into a basket. Fills it with
handfuls of fresh grass and sprigs of lavender that aren't yet blooming.

That night Mary dreams she's a bee. It's her twenty-sixth day on Earth—
almost the end of her life—and like all the days before, this one is a buzzing
symphony of nectar and of need.

Soolie in a Tree

We see Soolie outside the windows.
We see she's barefoot, just as she has been, every day, since third grade.
No one can make Soolie wear shoes: Not a principal a teacher a grandparent
the governor god or us. No one.

(Just look at Soolie's face when someone's scolding her: All she hears is
moonlight and new snow.)

Outside the window, Soolie climbs the slender trunk of a tree. A birch?
Maple? We haven't studied the names of trees in Biology.

Soolie is so small, she reminds us of a brown bird. A robin? A wren?
Something with drab wings. At any rate, she's supposed to be in school, not
perched in the leaves.

Why, Soolie? Why can't you be like us? Why can't you wear sweaters and
shoes in January? Why can't you sit in class like we're all doing?

Here we are in rows, on the other side of the windows. When the bell rings
we'll get up and move to our next classes. Some to Geometry, some to
Spanish, some to Government, and when the bell rings again we'll be right
where we're supposed to be, in our desks, faces to the front of the room,
learning.

That's our job. Until we graduate and get cars and jobs. That's what we'll be
doing.

But what about you, Soolie-Q, with your scrappy arms and little claws where
feet should be? What will your eyes of feathered clouds and milky stars see?

Sally in a Tangerine

Today I'm inside a tangerine.
How my pinched feet crave
to point and flex,
to spark tiny arias in tendons—

Oh tangerine, I've relished your scent,
but inside of you I'm rolled up tight, a snail
that never travels past its first leaf,
an embryo with my nose pressed to spongy knees—

Back in the womb today when I was just beginning to relish
the length and acuity of my bones (navicular, cuboid, talus!)
and the blossoming of heart and ribs
as storms of salt and hail
christened my skin.

2.

Pilgrim's Progress

*For Constance Hopkins, who sailed on the Mayflower with
her parents, married Nicholas Snow, and bore 12 children.*

Constance Snow, Constance Snow. A false name that settles on my spiked
shoulders like a white cotton shawl.

You might expect me to drag my muffled footsteps under a long gray gown.

Or maybe I should subvert myself to become the feather-blue blanket you
keep folded at the end of your bed?

Even now you frown, praying for the patience of a cold falcon as I bare my
teeth and flap my hands.

This is me, this is me:

   The scrape of a metal file across an old axe blade.
   Pans clashing in the ship's galley.
   The screech of violin strings when a bow touches them.

Beside me, a basket full of worn socks mutely beg to be mended.

Outside, gleaming crows caw through the smoke of thatched rooftops,
reveling in the music that rasps from their open mouths.

Origami

She is small
and colorful,
sometimes
shiny red
like a child's
Valentine
or bright green
like tree frogs
in spring;
other times
she's more complex,
tattooed
with white and blue
foot bridges, a pagoda,
a pregnant orange tree,
or delicate gold markings—
dashes and swirls—
that make poems
only she can read.

She is small
and thin enough
to fold,
first in half one way
then the other,
turning back her corners
then opening
her again,
in our hands, she becomes
a house,
a basket cupping
two strawberries,
a sky-blue kite
with no strings.

Some of our folds
are less precise,
leaving her lopsided—
like the time we turned her
into a one-eared fox—

and all this folding
and unfolding
has left her creased,
no matter how hard we try
to smooth her out again.
Still, we wonder
what else she might become.

Just last night I dreamed
she folded herself
into a new shape—
a white bird,
her long legs standing
on the edge of a pond,
a curved throat
and a cascade
of snowy feathers
down her back—
the bride's veil lifted,
her face finally revealed.
She had two swords for a beak
and when she dipped her head
into the still green water
she cut a fish in two,
stretched her neck,
and swallowed.

Hunter's Moon

In this bowl of moonlit earth, shadows float like silent wolves—
your scarlet coat the same shade as my chipped nail polish, your buttons
as gold as the gleam of new wanting, and the grass
here, so green—like a gift or a wound.
A confession for you:
I once took your tall boots and strutted up and down Main Street in them.
Imagine me, sauntering past the bank, the pharmacy, and into
the café where I ordered a soda (strawberry, because it's red and its letters
cup words like *brew, web, awe, star, was*).
I spilled a drop on one toe, then sat and admired
it like a jewel—tiny—roughly the size of an arrow's tip—
or the mole tucked into the crease of your left armpit (has anyone
other than me—and your mother—noticed how it resembles
a ladybug with extended wings?)
I see you now in this cathedral of moonlight,
raising your unblinking aim toward feathered trees
despite my hop and flap, my ruffle and caw. Hunter:
does your gallant hat ever slip off your head when you draw back your bow?
Blend of feathers and cedar branches: Again,
you have missed your target. And who will be here
to witness your fall—in the crumpled moonlight
of some tomorrow?

From the Imaginary Journals of a Kidnapped Heiress, part 1

Today I'm not

        Rebel
        Demon
        Victim
        Pig,
        Guerilla
        Turncoat
        Outlaw
        Liar,
        Leftist
        Convict
        Witness
        Rich

Today I'm a creature,

    breathing,

I'm bones
I'm skin

Lungs, arms, liver, blood

Teeth, nails, muscles, gut

                and at my core,   a heart—

        like any heart—

a rabbit
a lion,
a flower
a fist.

From the Imaginary Journals of a Kidnapped Heiress, part 2

Who exactly

      does it help

              if I

          agree

                 to despise

my

         self?

From the Imaginary Journals of a Kidnapped Heiress, part 3

Bless me,
Father,
for I have been
  sinned against

      (did I do wrong
      when I fought to live?)

I sat in darkness
with wrists bound
and gummed new words
from a pistol's mouth

they gave me scripts
and shaved my hair
included me in combat drills—

push-ups
targets
grenade pins

      starved
      gagged
        berated:
        'bitch'

        raped
        armed
      fondled
      kissed

captors captive
arrested, killed
I wore cuffs
and crossed myself

fell from my gelding
like a star—
  puppet, pietà,
  cradled by guards

toss a coin, choose a side
seven heads, countless wigs,
spray of bullets
fugitive—

one thing here is for certain:
my shorn hair's grown long—
  my shiny, blond
  curtain.

Princess, Seated

Reflections on Pisanello's "Portrait of a Princess of the House of Este"

Behind me you see brushstrokes
and butterfly wings, like black-eyed lemons
and tangerines—pinned but still alive,
as if the walls are moving,
an inhale of drapes in a breeze.
In the foreground, me, thinking:

Inside my father's house,
with bare white neck stretched long,
I sit and become a marble pillar without breath—

not breathless, as in running across
a field, sting of bumblebee swelling
on my fingerprint, the clear sky
reeling above my head as I extend
arms and spin, held steady by
the firm blur of pines on all sides
and the galloping scent
of an incantation:

I will not join your dance—
I will not wear the colors of your convent
I will not murmur your parchment prayers
under the pale stones of your crumbled arch—

I'd sooner be a wall
of brilliant flickering wings
or a small flame
wavering on the tip
of a candle's wick—

one puff and I'm gone—

Isn't that how it is for everyone?

3.

The Ride

Inside this coach—
half-pumpkin, half-carriage—
the air is ripe.
I lean back against
one thick curved wall,
and its dampness seeps
into my borrowed dress
so that the ivory silk
clings like a second skin.
My heavy hair is slipping
from its snug pins—I feel it
curl around my face—while
over my head a moist seed
hangs by a yellow thread.
As the carriage bumps its way
over rocks and twigs, I watch
the seed swing this way and that,
like a pendulum gone wild. I open
my palm, and the seed drops into it.
Ahead, the ballroom waits,
lit with candles and the pulsing
of my own heart beats—
no more breathy songs
smothered in soap bubbles,
no more pretend partners,
no more tentative shadow steps
in the confines of my kitchen—
when the carriage comes to a stop,
I don't wait for the coachman.
I push open the door
and step into my night.

To Whom It May Concern

In the mirror I see the old me—
white me (snow white, actually),
cooking for my seven friends
then scrubbing their latrine
while whistling.

*

Contrary to popular belief, I was in no hurry to be rescued
from the glass casket they built for me.

In fact, I was having the best dream—on top of a mountain,
away from everyone—friends, prince, evil queen—
just rock and snow and me, on the brink
of understanding something when the prince
galloped up on his panting horse,
lifted the clear lid and hovered
over my frozen lips.

*

As a husband, he's fine. He's busy.
Me, not so much.
Everything here is so clean.

Now, when I dream, my callused fingers grip
a splintered broomstick. Or I plunge
a scrub brush in a bucket
of scalding suds.

They smell like juniper, I think, although I don't know
what juniper smells like. Or what it looks like, either;
I never went to school. Can't, in fact, read or write.
My maid is taking dictation now. She smirks and says,
Don't worry, I'll leave nothing out.

*

I've learned a little in this life:
A perfect red apple can be poison.
A hunter's heart may be softer than it seems.
Sisterhood is sometimes a pipe dream.

I go by instinct.

And memory:
The shadows of my face reflected in a pool of wash water on the floor.
The sky opening in my breastbone as I swept my friends' glowing hearth.

The Thirteenth Fairy

I like my spells
and spinning smoke.

She's a princess
who slept for a century.
Now, suddenly, she's awake
and loves everyone—
even I am forgiven:
End of story.

She ventures to my hut,
says she sees past
my molting robe
and rotten-kernel teeth.
She says,
you once had a newborn heart
that cradled a soft beat
like moth's wings rising from a leaf.

Ha!
I open my mouth wide
and the flames of my forked tongue
lash her cheek.

Poor thing.
She thinks she can massage
the knots of rage from my shoulder blades,
make me sigh and chirp and curl.

The little fool pictures me,
her enemy, the bad, bad fairy,
relenting, on bended knee,
offering to bring her mint and honey
or to prick my finger on a spindle
in exchange for her kiss
on my thatched head.

What an imagination this girl has.
That, I believe, could be
her real curse,
not me.

Sighs of the Mermaid

Say a mermaid meets a man
   who's handsome,
      and drowning,

say she swims him to shore and gets him breathing again,

          say when Handsome opens his eyes,

she instantly grows a pair of legs,
   helps him home,
      helps him out of his sodden swimming trunks
         enjoys his kisses and a soft bath scented with mint
and lavender;

              so many things to like
on land with him—
the aroma of fresh toast coming from the kitchen,
        restaurants, candles, a tablecloth,

    she learns to pour pools of pale green olive oil
onto white plates and let pieces of warm bread soak it up
            like a sea sponge—

so strange to sit, though,
   while eating
          what an effort not to undulate
her legs beneath the table

     —and where are the tiny teacup-shaped barnacles,
        the lacy bouquets of algae, the pale pink shrimp
that once tiptoed

          over her own fins?—

while he's at the office, she goes to the track and finds she can't
        run as fast as she could (once) swim
   now

she sits on the couch and reads help wanteds and realizes she must
   a) learn how to drive
   b) explore the depths of data entry or
   c) serve ice cream

sometimes he feeds her strawberries from his garden—
             how can he know
                        she longs for the slick, green taste
of salt?

sometimes she awakens in the airless night to find
   his leg flung over her like an anchor from an iron ship

                        while minutes and hours wave by
             like an underwater ballet

she stares at the ceiling and imagines him
             sailing off on some new journey—
                        would her fins
grow back if his fingers got tangled
                        in another woman's hair?

             sometimes

                        a whisper of flame flickers in her heart

      if only it would ignite into a full-fledged conflagration—

      as long as she doesn't weep—
             a single tear could turn his house

into a quiet pond, and she, like a shimmering koi,
             could end up circling just below its surface
                        for a hundred years
             or more.

Not Me

If only I could remember what it was—
my name before they dubbed me
Cinderella.
It sounds so pretty, doesn't it?
Like lady slippers and gilded leaves.
You could almost forget it was meant to mock and burn
the tender heart of a seed.

Can you blame me if I prefer
the company of men

or birds
or mice
or lizards?

Living where you're not wanted
is like walking on broken glass—
I tried to make myself light
so the shards wouldn't slice
my tender soles.

Sometimes
I could even do it—
hold my curved shoulders back, fill my lungs with breath
and feel myself floating, a cloud without brain, stomach or skin.

Inevitably, though, I'd blink,
forget to sing:
The electricity of fresh-cut flesh
makes it hard to think of other things.

So yes, I took all the help I could get—
the spell, the pumpkin, the dress
and him—
don't laugh—
I could see what hid beneath his silk and crown.
Not at the dance,
but on that first night
when we knelt by the fireplace
and anointed each other
with warm ash.

4.

Sally in a Painting

Sally lives in a picture of her own making,
with tempera laid on so thick it never dries.
Maybe it even drips, leaving big dots
that turn the floor into a game of Twister—
right hand near the stove,
left hip jutting toward the front door.
Sally says the paint smells of pine trees
and pickles and a bee burying its tongue
in a copper chrysanthemum.
Squint, she says, and you may find
a wispy smile in the cerulean swirls perched
on the pale tips of pink needles.
Above, puce wings refuse to be tethered
by the geometry of paper, frame or canvas—
blink and they've taken flight.
In their place, the shoulder
of a shadowed pond where priests
and princesses alike bathe in the scent
of cigarettes and fresh mud.

Romance of the Alien

after Sonya Kelly's "How to Keep an Alien"

Back at school,
rehearsing the bob and wince
of yet another dance sequence.
In my throat, the cobwebs of a midlife crisis compete
with the tick-tock of tears dropping from the gilded chandelier:
I, too, am ridiculous.
Bounce, bounce, twirl and bow
between the same velvet curtains and the ring of rosy lights,
embracing the bouquet of my latest near-miss.
All that time indoors,
collecting paychecks and limp applause,
and I still can't swim.
But in the moonlight, my silhouette is an alien,
a new friend.
Am I listening?
I won't be alone
again.

Sally as a Drake

At night, Sally and Rodrigo
tell each other things.

Rodrigo says his grandmother could stir
sopa de lima and smoke a cigarette
and touch his head at the same time.
He says he once dreamt
a rose vine wrapped its woody arms
around his grandmother's house
so that no one could get in or out.

Sally stretches her legs across the rug
so that the soles of her Chinese slippers
meet the worn soles of Rodrigo's boots.

Sally says she pictures her grandmother
in a pilled cardigan, a shimmering fleck
of onion skin stuck to the sleeve,
face moist from the steam
of a beige pudding.

Lightning and a wisp of candle smoke.
Rodrigo nudges Sally's knee with his.
Which one is your grandmother? he asks.
The lightning or the breeze?

Sally thinks the whole sky—
clouds and stars and scattered light—
is made of ancestors.
She imagines herself and Rodrigo
as a pair of mallards. Sometimes
she'll be the dun-colored female
foraging beside a pond while Rodrigo,
the drake, stands watch. Other times
he'll be the one to hunt for bugs and berries
and bits of damp grass while she holds
her gleaming head high to listen and to guard
all they love.

Soolie and the Art of Being

I hum along the faded corridors and slip into
the diva's dressing room where I flick my wings
in the tunnel of her kimono's silken sleeve—
I leave my footprints in her spilled face powder
and wear her silver eye shadow like a pair of iridescent shoes—
I glimpse my flash and glimmer in her bright mirror
then buzz through the shifting heat of the auditorium
to circle zip dash dive over the sweet sticky hairdos
of the ladies in their capes and pearls—
I land on the smooth black knee of the flutist
then soar to the tip of the conductor's baton,
where together we stir the air, gathering a basilica
of notes then releasing them to mingle and pulse—
I burrow in the thick folds of the velvet curtains
before skimming through the dust suspended in a beam of light
as I shape the perfect curves of figure eights
to the beat of the applause rising from the theater seats
and my belief this is the way things are for everybody:
art and motion, ecstasy, ovation, *encore*!

A five-time Pushcart nominee, **Linda Ferguson** is an award-winning writer of poetry, fiction and essays. She's the author of two previous poetry chapbooks, *Baila Conmigo,* which was published by Dancing Girl Press, and *Of the Forest,* which was the 2nd place winner of The Poetry Box Chapbook Prize, 2021. As a writing teacher, she has a passion for helping students find their voice and explore new territory.

bylindaferguson.blogspot.com
@ljdferguson.1